HOW TO BE AN
ASTRONAUT

Amanda Li

Illustrated by Mike Phillips

MACMILLAN CHILDREN'S BOOKS

First published 2006 by Macmillan Children's Books
a division of Macmillan Publishers Limited
20 New Wharf Road, London N1 9RR
Basingstoke and Oxford
www.panmacmillan.com

Associated companies throughout the world

ISBN-13: 978-0-330-44614-2
ISBN-10: 0-330-44614-2

Text copyright © Amanda Li 2006
Illustrations copyright © Mike Phillips 2006

1 3 5 7 9 8 6 4 2

A CIP catalogue record for this book is available from
the British Library.

Design by John Fordham

Printed and bound in China

Picture credits:
Science Museum/Science & Society Picture Library
Pages 4, 14, 16 (bottom), 17 (bottom), 21 (centre), 24 (top).
NASA/Science & Society Picture Library
Pages 1, 2, 3, 5, 6, 7, 8, 9, 11, 12, 13, 17 (top and centre), 18, 19, 20, 21 (top and bottom),
22, 24 (bottom), 25, 26, 28, 29, 30, 31.
ITR Tass/Science & Society Picture Library
Page 16 (top).

363

CONTENTS

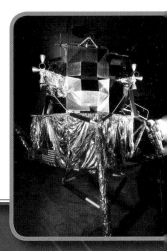

science
museum

SO, YOU WANT TO BE AN ASTRONAUT?

Many people dream of journeying into space. It's the ultimate adventure, the thrill of a lifetime. But some people turn their dreams into reality – they train to become astronauts.

The kinds of things that astronauts might do are truly mind-blowing. When else would you get the chance to be blasted above the atmosphere? To go to Mars, where no human has ever gone before? To see your home, Earth, as a tiny planet far, far away? It really is an amazing job, but it's not an easy one. Even the selection process is tough. You'll need to be intelligent, fit and have the right kind of experience and personality to make it on to that space rocket. But if you do, the rewards are great – after all, you'll be getting paid for doing the most thrilling job in the world!

Looking for a job that's 'out of this world'?

☐ Are you a team player? ☐ Are you physically fit?
☐ Do you have a sense of adventure?
☐ Are you interested in maths or science-related subjects?
☐ Do you think you have good judgement?
☐ Would you like a job that involves long-distance travel?

If you can tick all the boxes above, then you might have what it takes to join our space-training programme and become a fully fledged astronaut.

ДЕНЬ КОСМОНАВТ
СССР

Yuri Gargarin, 1961

THE FIRST ASTRONAUTS

The Russian cosmonaut **Yuri Gagarin** made history when he completed the first orbit of the Earth in the spacecraft *Vostok* on 12 April 1961. Up until this time no one had been sure if it was possible for a human to survive a journey into space, so the news was greeted with huge excitement by the world.

The American space agency, **NASA** (National Aeronautics and Space Administration), had also been training its first astronauts – a group of seven men – for a historic space voyage. One of them, **John Glenn**, became the first American to orbit the Earth, on 20 February 1962. Both Gagarin and Glenn were celebrated as national heroes.

The original seven NASA astronauts were all military pilots, but today's astronauts come from all kinds of different backgrounds. NASA's current group of would-be space adventurers includes teachers, doctors, scientists and engineers. Anyone can apply for astronaut training – but only a few make it through …

Astro Fact
The word 'astronaut' actually means 'star sailor' in Latin.
The Russian word for astronaut is 'cosmonaut'.

The 'Mercury Seven' astronauts, 1959. The seven test pilots chosen in April 1959 to participate in Project Mercury, NASA's first manned space project. They are *(front row left to right)* Walter Schirra, Donald Slayton, John Glenn, Scott Carpenter; *(back row left to right)* Alan Shepard, Virgil Grissom and Gordon Cooper.

GETTING OFF THE GROUND

First things first. If you're serious about a career in space, you'll need to know which type of astronaut you want to be.

Pilot Astronaut

You're responsible for controlling and piloting the spacecraft. With enough experience you might one day be promoted to the position of **commander**, taking charge of the vehicle and crew and having ultimate responsibility for the safety and success of the flight.

Mission Specialist

You're responsible for all operations on the craft apart from piloting. Part of your job is to perform **EVA** – extravehicular activity – which means you go 'space walking' outside the craft in order to do your work.

Some missions offer an extra job opportunity:

Payload Specialist

The **payload** is the cargo capacity of the craft, which may include scientific instruments and experiments. As a payload specialist you will have knowledge of a certain area, such as physics or medical science, that is needed for the mission and you will perform experiments and do research on board the craft. You will probably come from a research or university background and, although you're not an astronaut, will train alongside the crew.

Michael Collins, Command Module Pilot on *Apollo 11*, the first mission to the moon in 1969

Astronaut **Bruce McCandless** on the first space walk using the Manned Manoeuvring Unit, 1984. The MMU has small gas thrusters that enable an astronaut to move around outside the space shuttle without a tether.

MAKING THE GRADE

Hopeful astronauts have to meet certain requirements to have a chance of being selected. The first is that you have to be an adult – sadly, young people aren't allowed to travel into space (but one day, who knows?). However, there is a lot you can do to start preparing for your future career right now. Keeping fit is very important and you'll also need to make sure that you're studying the right kinds of subjects (see below).

Different space agencies around the world have their own requirements for astronaut candidates, but they're all very similar:

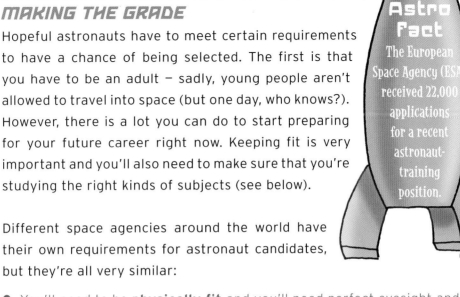

Astro Fact
The European Space Agency (ESA) received 22,000 applications for a recent astronaut-training position.

- You'll need to be **physically fit** and you'll need perfect eyesight and healthy blood pressure. You must also meet certain weight and height standards. For some of the tests, rotating chairs, pressure chambers and aircraft are used.

- A university **degree** in science, engineering or maths is essential.

- **Flying experience** is welcomed for all types of astronaut but absolutely vital if you're applying to be a pilot astronaut. For this job, you need to be a fully trained pilot with at least 1,000 hours experience of piloting a jet aircraft.

Candidates are evaluated over a week of interviews and tests. Many people have the right qualifications and experience – but not everyone has the right kind of personality.

All astronaut trainees need to be determined and patient because a great deal of hard work lies ahead. For every hour they will spend in space, hundreds of hours of training will be completed beforehand.

ASTRONAUT PERSONALITY PROFILE
- Good at working as part of a team (very important when you are a member of a mission crew)
- Excellent memory
- Good concentration
- Highly motivated and flexible
- Ability to get along with people

YOUR BODY IN SPACE

Our bodies are 'glued' to Earth by an invisible force called gravity. It is a force of attraction between objects that affects everything in the universe. And it is the gravitational attraction of the earth that gives us our weight and makes things fall to the ground if we drop them.

But when astronauts orbit the earth they experience a very unusual sensation – weightlessness. In photos of them 'swimming' around their spaceship they appear to be floating. However, this is not what is actually happening – in fact, their bodies are falling. The astronauts feel as if they are floating because the spacecraft around them is falling at exactly the same rate. So why are they (and the craft) not hitting the ground? And what causes the weightlessness?

Members of the crew of *Discovery* Mission 51-G, experiencing weightlessness in the pressurized area of the shuttle.

GOING INTO FREEFALL

When you throw a stone it moves in two ways at the same time. It travels horizontally through the air and it also moves vertically, down to the ground (due to the effect of gravity). Sooner or later the stone hits the ground. Now try to imagine a giant who can throw a stone so incredibly hard horizontally that, as the stone moves, the curve it makes precisely follows the curve of the Earth's surface. It never hits the ground.

EARTH

This is exactly what is happening to our spacecraft. It is travelling at such a speed that it goes into 'freefall' or orbit. And when an object is in 'free fall', a state called zero gravity (more accurately known as **microgravity**) occurs. Objects become virtually weightless, because the effect of gravity is reduced the further away from the Earth they are.

YOUR BODY AND ZERO GRAVITY

Astronauts who stay in zero gravity for weeks or months find that it has a noticeable impact on their bodies:

- Their bones lose density and become thinner because they are not carrying their normal weight.

- Some muscles lose mass because there is no resistance – they do not have the Earth's gravitational force to constantly push against.

On Earth blood tends to pool in your feet – if you stand on your head your face goes red, because the blood (which usually goes down into your feet) is now trying to fall into your head. Being in zero-G equalizes the distribution of blood in your body so your bodily fluids no longer try to fall into your feet. This causes your face to become puffy and swollen-looking and your legs to become thinner.

- Astronauts can counteract the effects of zero gravity on their bones and muscles by doing exercises, such as running on a treadmill or rowing on a machine. Just like a gym on planet Earth – only in zero-G you have to be strapped in to stop yourself floating away!

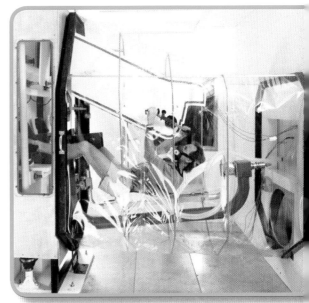
Exercising in zero-G

Astrofact
One unpleasant effect of zero gravity is space motion sickness. Many astronauts feel nauseous, but the symptoms usually wear off after a few days.

IT'S TRAINING TIME

So you've got the qualifications, filled in the forms and are now raring to fly the shuttle. You'll be in a specialist centre doing basic training for one year, and if you're successful you'll go on to more advanced training, tailored towards becoming either a pilot or a mission specialist.

Back to the Classroom

Get those textbooks out – your studies will include physics, maths, computer sciences, astronomy, meteorology (the science of the atmosphere and the weather) and oceanography. Navigation skills and first aid will also be vital.

Flying High

You will be trained to fly a jet aircraft, learning about safety and how to eject from a craft in an emergency landing. Would-be pilot astronauts will fly for longer and will practise in a **shuttle training aircraft**.

Shuttle Simulation

You'll get acquainted with the **space shuttle**, a reusable winged spacecraft for transporting astronauts. Life-size mock-ups of the craft will be used so you can practise on 'real' controls and displays.

Survival Skills

Water survival skills are essential, as you may have to bail out of your craft during take-off or landing – and there's a good chance that you'll splashdown on water. But you'll need to know how to survive in all kinds of conditions, from scorching deserts to freezing ice sheets. Techniques for building shelters and finding food and water should keep you alive until you are picked up.

Sharon Christa McAuliffe experiences weightlessness aboard NASA's KC 135 'zero-gravity' aircraft. McAuliffe was representing the Teacher in Space Project. She was aboard the STS 51-L/ *Challenger* when it exploded during take-off on 28 January 1986, claiming the lives of the crew.

BEING WEIGHTLESS

Here comes the fun part – the different ways of learning how to cope in a weightless environment:

The 'Vomit Comet'

This is the nickname given to the specially modified **KC-135 'zero-gravity' aircraft**, a plane that creates the conditions of zero gravity by flying upwards and downwards in gigantic curves. At a certain point during the curve, you feel the sensation of weightlessness and will 'float' for about twenty seconds, an event which is repeated throughout the flight. This is your chance to practise using flight equipment as well as eating and drinking.

Underwater EVA

You'll be able to experience weightlessness for longer periods in the **neutral-buoyancy tank**, a deep unit full of water that is ideal for practising 'space walks' while wearing a pressurized suit.

Hanging Around

Another way of getting used to 'floating' is by being suspended from a large harness. There is also a special mechanical chair called the **5DF** (Five Degrees of Freedom), that lifts you up in the air, allowing you to move in all kinds of directions, just as you would in orbit.

More Freaky Machines

- Practise 'bunny hopping' on the moon by being strapped into a specially designed chair that springs up and down.

- The **multi-axis wheel** (or centrifuge machine) is a huge sphere that simulates the spinning that can occur in space during a mission.

Astro Fact

Could you swim three lengths of a 25-metre pool wearing a flight suit and gym shoes? All trainees have to do this.

ENTER THE DANGER ZONE

Reaching and exploring in space is very dangerous. Each mission must be meticulously planned in order to minimize the risks astronauts face.

The Launch

A rocket is launched when its explosive fuel is ignited. The combustion (rate of burning) is controlled and enables the rocket to lift off the ground and accelerate towards space. A fault in the rocket will cause an uncontrolled explosion, as happened when the space shuttle *Challenger* blew up in 1986.

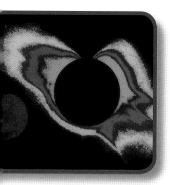

Radiation

The earth's magnetic field protects us from most of the dangerous radiation that comes from the sun and from deep space. Astronauts are at risk from this radiation and must be protected from it as much as possible.

Space Walking

Leaving the 'safety' of the spacecraft or space station is particularly dangerous: there is the risk of floating away, so the astronauts are normally tethered; and their space- suits may be punctured by the fast-moving specks of dust and debris that orbit the Earth, so the suits are strengthened to resist these impacts.

Re-entry

When a space mission is finished the astronauts must return to Earth through the atmosphere. They will be travelling at least 28,000 kmh (17,000 mph) and their spacecraft's surface will heat up as the air is squashed in front of it. If they come in too steeply they will burn up; if they come in too gradually they will bounce off and back out into space.

Launch and re-entry are the riskiest moments of the mission. Here a space shuttle is shown taking off on a successful mission.

The prototype **Personal Rescue Enclosure** (PRE) was a 100-cm (34-inch) ball that contained its own short-term life-support systems. The PRE was never actually produced for use on the space shuttle.

OTHER WORLDS

When astronauts travel to other worlds they will encounter many more hazards. Their distance from Earth will make it even more important to plan each part of the mission.

Distant Worlds

Six missions landed astronauts on the moon between 1969 and 1972. If anything had gone wrong on the surface, the astronauts would have died: there was no way in which a rescue mission could have been sent. On Mars, the astronauts' isolation will be greater still: the astronauts will have to be able to deal with any emergency and any sickness that occur during the eighteen-month round trip to and from the red planet.

Communicating with Earth

Radio communications to and from the moon took about three seconds each; those for Mars will take up to 20 minutes. It will be almost impossible for the astronauts and mission control to talk, especially if the astronauts need help and advice immediately.

Martian Dust

The moon is dusty, but there is no wind so the dust mostly stays on the ground. On Mars, there are frequent dust storms in its carbon dioxide-rich atmosphere and dust could clog up vital electrical and life-support systems.

Mars viewed by a *Viking* orbiter, 1976

Going Mad

On a space mission it is just you, your few crew mates and space. The *Apollo* astronauts were back with their families and friends after less than a fortnight. Any moods or quarrels on board would soon be forgotten when they returned to Earth. On a mission to Mars you will be cooped up in your spacecraft or in your lander for months and months.

YOUR MISSION BEGINS

Explorers have ventured out to satisfy their curiosity about the world for centuries. The only difference now is that we can explore off-planet too.

Hundreds of space missions have taken place over the years, ever since the moment in October 1957 when the very first satellite, *Sputnik 1*, was launched by the Russians. This marked the beginning of the 'space age' – a period of time, particularly during the 1960s and 1970s, when huge advances in space technology were made and many important space 'firsts' took place.

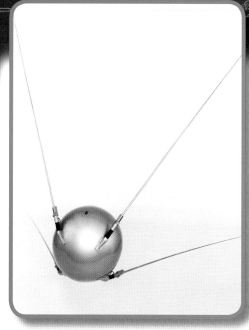

The *Sputnik 1* satellite

Manned or Unmanned?

Unmanned missions are craft that travel without humans on board. They are lighter and more fuel-efficient than manned craft, so they can travel much further. They can also venture to parts of the solar system that manned space flight cannot yet reach. The Russians never managed to land cosmonauts on the moon, but sent the unmanned *Luna 9* to a soft landing in 1966 – three years before the Americans sent their astronauts. These days we are sending robotic **probes** to Mars to conduct experiments even though we are many years away from being able to send astronauts to Mars.

Human space flight was started as part of the 'Cold War', when the Soviet Union and the United States of America competed to see who could do most in space. For most of the 1960s the two nations raced to land a man on the moon – the US won in 1969! Since then US astronauts and Russian cosmonauts have continued to work in space, often helping each other to carry out scientific experiments and build space stations.

A replica of the **Mars Sojourner** micro-rover, launched in 1996. Roughly the size of a microwave oven, the rover was powered by a solar panel and remotely controlled by scientists on Earth.

THE FIRST SPACE WALKER

The story of this mission proves that the survival skills learned during astronaut training are essential:

Astro Fact

International Space Station astronauts Susan Helms and Jim Voss made the longest space walk in history on 11 March 2001 – 8 hours and 56 minutes.

In 1965 Russian **Aleksei Leonov** was the first cosmonaut to venture outside a craft and perform a space walk. The event was fraught with danger. After 23 minutes in space his suit had inflated so much that he could not re-enter the airlock. He had to open a valve to reduce the pressure inside the suit – a difficult and dangerous job – but finally made it back into his capsule, suffering from heat exhaustion. It had been a close call.

On its return, Leonov's capsule, *Voskhod 2*, landed in the forests on the Russian Ural mountains, but its locator antennae were damaged and the rescue team was unable to reach the crew until the next day. Leonov and his colleague built a fire to keep warm, but were attacked by packs of wolves. Retreating to the capsule, they had to spend the night holding the hatch shut against the wolves.

ASTRONAUT ACHIEVEMENTS

Astronauts are brave people. Imagine being the very first person to get in a capsule and orbit the Earth when no one else has proved that it can be done. Here are the important – and daring – human mission 'firsts' of space history:

12 April 1961

Yuri Gagarin is the first human in space. He is also the first person to orbit the Earth, spending 108 minutes aboard the capsule *Vostok 1*.

20 February 1962

John Glenn is the first American to orbit the Earth in his capsule, *Friendship 7*. He orbits the Earth three times, taking four hours and 55 minutes.

16 June 1963

The Russians send the first woman, **Valentina Tereshkova**, into space, aboard *Vostok 6*. They study the effect of space travel on the female body.

12 October 1964

The first **multi-manned space flight** (more than one person on board) takes place. Three Russian cosmonauts fly 16 orbits of the earth in 24 hours aboard *Voskhod.* They also fly without space suits for the first time (there was no room to wear them).

18 March 1965

The first extravehicular activity takes place. Russian **Aleksei Leonov** space walks for about 12 minutes.

21 July 1969

American **Neil Armstrong** is the first person to set foot on the moon, stepping off the lunar module *Eagle*. His colleague, **Edwin 'Buzz' Aldrin** (pictured), collects lunar samples for analysis.

17 July 1975

The first **international space mission** takes place. The American *Apollo* spacecraft, carrying a crew of three, docks with a Russian *Soyuz* spacecraft with its crew of two and their commanders shake hands. It's a historic moment for US–Soviet relations.

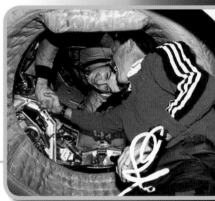

24 June 1983

Sally Ride, America's first woman in space, returns safely to earth after a six-day flight in the *Challenger* space shuttle.

18 May 1991

Britain's first astronaut, **Helen Sharman**, takes off as part of the crew aboard the *Soyuz TM-12*, on a scientific mission called Project Juno.

28 April 2001

The Russian craft *Soyuz TM-32* is taken to the International Space Station. The first space tourist, American **Dennis Tito**, pays 20 million dollars to go on the voyage.

Astro Fact

For many years there was intense competition between the Soviet Union and the United States – the 'Space Race'. Both wanted to achieve the all-important 'firsts' in space.

AN ASTRONAUT'S WORK

Being an astronaut is not exactly a nine-to-five job. And whether you're on a mission or based on the ground, there's no chance of getting bored.

A technician examines a research satellite.

Mission Tasks

- **Flying** space vehicles
- Carrying out scientific **research**, such as testing new products for use in space
- **Maintaining**, testing and repairing equipment
- **Operating** the remote manipulator system to place satellites into orbit (or retrieve them)
- **Construction** – the International Space Station has been built by astronauts
- **Monitoring** the payload (the cargo) of the craft

Mission Control as it looked in the heyday of *Apollo*.

Ground Tasks

- Providing **ground support**
- Thoroughly **testing** all equipment
- **Preparing** for future missions – astronauts need to practise rarely used skills such as shuttle flying and EVA

Working the Robot 'Arm'

As a mission specialist aboard NASA's space shuttle you might get the job of operating the **Remote Manipulator System** (RMS) – a 15-metre long robotic arm attached to the outside of the shuttle. It has six joints and is controlled by an operator inside the shuttle with the use of computerized joysticks. The robot arm can make extremely complex movements and is used for satellite deployment and retrieval and general servicing tasks, such as repairing the **Hubble Space Telescope**.

The robot arm aboard the shuttle *Discovery* manoeuvres the Hubble Space Telescope into position.

ASAT SMMR WATER VAPOR
LY 7 – OCTOBER 10, 1978

What Is a Satellite?

A satellite is any object that orbits another object. Artificial satellites are man-made objects, structures that we place in space for a variety of reasons. They are incredibly useful in our everyday lives; for example, weather satellites help us forecast the weather and telecommunications satellites transmit signals to our radios and televisions.

When astronaut **Sally Ride** flew aboard the shuttle in 1983 she used the RMS to retrieve a satellite package of experiments from space for the very first time, paving the way for repairing satellites in orbit. Sally had helped design the robotic arm.

A Building Site in Space

402 km above our heads is the largest artificial satellite currently orbiting our planet – the **International Space Station** (ISS). In order to construct it, astronauts had to work as builders, hauling supplies, connecting power lines and bolting components together using robotic cranes and power tools – all done in zero gravity while wearing bulky spacesuits. It's very different to a building site on Earth, where if you drop something it falls to the ground – rather than floating off.

An artist's impression of the International Space Station

Astro Fact

The ISS is a complex and expensive project that will need even more work if it is to be completed. The nations involved hope that we will one day see the world's largest space research facility in use.

METERS

There's a huge rumble and a sudden blast, accompanied by clouds of flame and gas. A space rocket has launched.

How Do Rockets Work?

A massive amount of energy is needed to launch something into space, and a rocket can only take off if it has enough force to propel it upwards. Conventional rockets work by a force called **propulsion**. The rocket is pushed forward because material is streaming out of the back of it, just as a blown-up balloon will shoot off if you suddenly release it. With rockets, however, superheated gases are pushed out. These gases are formed by fuel burning in the presence of oxygen, or a substance called an oxidizer.

The principle of rocket propulsion is based on the famous scientist Isaac Newton's third law:

The 1962 launch of the *Mercury Friendship 7* mission with John Glenn on board

For every action, there is an equal and opposite reaction.

In the case of a rocket, the craft pushes burning fuel downwards, and the fuel pushes upward on the rocket with an equal but opposite force. The force must be powerful enough to overcome the rocket's weight and accelerate it up into the sky and beyond.

The unmanned spacecraft *Voyager 1* launches from Cape Canaveral in Florida.

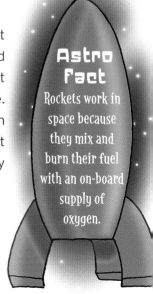

Astro Fact

Rockets work in space because they mix and burn their fuel with an on-board supply of oxygen.

Robert H. Goddard at the first flight of a liquid propellant rocket, in 1926

ROCKETING THROUGH HISTORY

- No one is quite sure when the first rockets were invented but we know that the ancient **Chinese** used rockets as weapons about a thousand years ago – bamboo tubes filled with gunpowder.

- In the 17th century **Newton** developed his three laws of physical motion, which help describe how rockets work.

- In the 19th century **Sir William Congreve** developed war rockets that were used in the Napoleonic Wars and the American War of Independence.

- In 1898 a Russian teacher called **Konstantin Tsiolkovsky** first suggested that humans might be able to use rockets to travel to space. His ideas were incredibly advanced for his time.

The V2 rocket

- In the 1940s the **V2** rocket – the first long-range rocket, which was powerful enough to destroy a building – was developed by German scientists and used against Britain during the Second World War. After the war America and the Soviet Union both realized the V2's potential and worked separately to develop the technology for use in space.

Can a Rocket Be Reused?

Unfortunately not. Rockets can blast you into space but they can't bring you down again. Astronauts need to enter a smaller capsule that breaks off from the main rocket. The rocket itself burns up, so it can never be used again. The **space shuttle** was a turning point in history because it was the first reusable craft. The first shuttle took off in 1981 and many flights have taken place since.

The space shuttle, the first reusable spacecraft

SUPER SPACE SHUTTLES

Rockets are still used for space travel but they come at a huge cost, as an entirely new rocket must be built for every mission. There is another way for astronauts to travel – by space shuttle. NASA created this part rocket, part aeroplane to be the world's first reusable spacecraft.

There are three parts to the shuttle. Only one part, the fuel tank, cannot be used again:

1. **Booster rockets** – these fall into the sea minutes after launch and are retrieved.

2. **External fuel tank** – the fuel to power the launch is soon used up and the tank is allowed to break up in the atmosphere.

3. **Orbiter** – the space plane carries the crew and cargo and flies back to Earth.

The Flight of a Shuttle

Launched with the aid of powerful rocket boosters, the shuttle blasts off from its launch pad, disposing of these rocket boosters soon after take-off. These are closely followed by the external fuel tank. The orbiter alone is left to complete the mission. Once the mission is accomplished, the orbiter flies back incredibly fast, entering the atmosphere at around 28,000 kmh (17,000 mph). It needs to slow down very quickly in order to make a safe runway landing.

FLIGHT DECK: WHERE THE ASTRONAUTS ARE LOCATED. THE SHUTTLE IS PILOTED FROM HERE

The shuttle takes a flight crew of four and has capacity for three passengers. There are currently three shuttle orbiters in the US – *Discovery*, *Atlantis* and *Endeavour*.

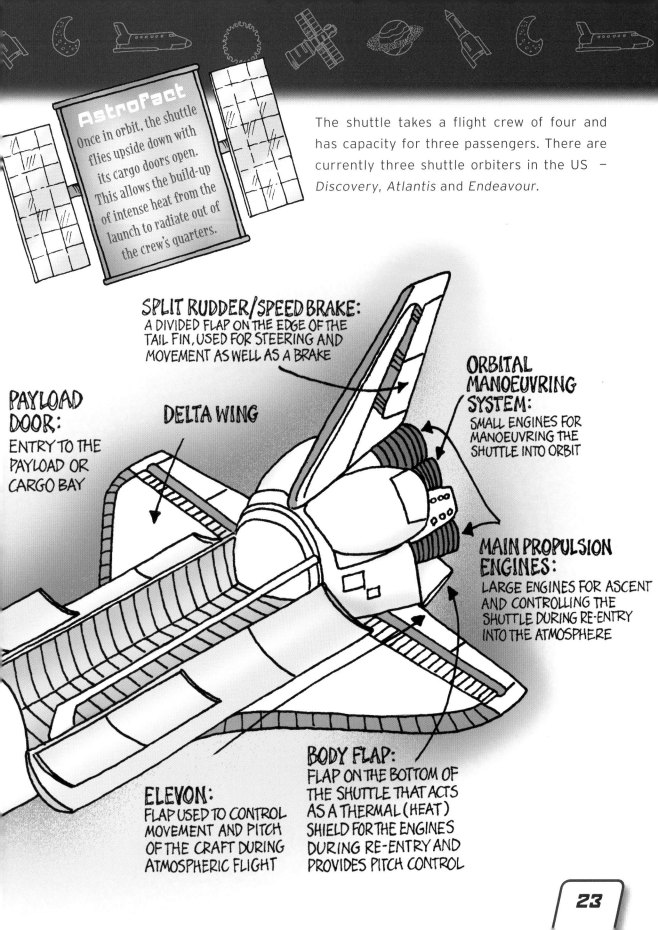

SPLIT RUDDER/SPEED BRAKE:
A DIVIDED FLAP ON THE EDGE OF THE TAIL FIN, USED FOR STEERING AND MOVEMENT AS WELL AS A BRAKE

ORBITAL MANOEUVRING SYSTEM:
SMALL ENGINES FOR MANOEUVRING THE SHUTTLE INTO ORBIT

PAYLOAD DOOR:
ENTRY TO THE PAYLOAD OR CARGO BAY

DELTA WING

MAIN PROPULSION ENGINES:
LARGE ENGINES FOR ASCENT AND CONTROLLING THE SHUTTLE DURING RE-ENTRY INTO THE ATMOSPHERE

ELEVON:
FLAP USED TO CONTROL MOVEMENT AND PITCH OF THE CRAFT DURING ATMOSPHERIC FLIGHT

BODY FLAP:
FLAP ON THE BOTTOM OF THE SHUTTLE THAT ACTS AS A THERMAL (HEAT) SHIELD FOR THE ENGINES DURING RE-ENTRY AND PROVIDES PITCH CONTROL

LIFE IN SPACE

Being in orbit is incredibly exciting, but you still need to eat, sleep and do all the everyday things that happen on Earth. But how will you manage it, hundreds of kilometres up in space?

Zero-gravity Dining

Imagine trying to spear a potato that keeps floating off your plate! This potential problem has been solved by some ingenious packaging ideas. You'll use a special meal tray that can be attached to the wall or strapped to your lap. In it you'll find a selection of tasty foods that are packaged in sealed pouches, cans and cups. All of them are easily cut or ripped open, to be eaten directly from the package.

Much of the food is dehydrated (the moisture has been taken out in order to conserve weight on the flight) so you'll need to add water to it. The package can then be heated up in an oven if necessary.

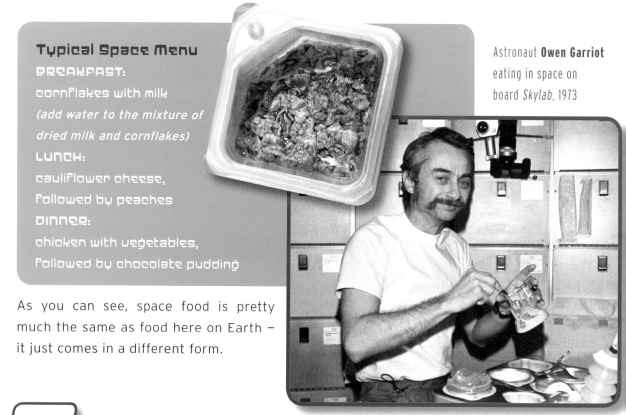

Typical Space Menu
BREAKFAST:
cornflakes with milk
(add water to the mixture of dried milk and cornflakes)
LUNCH:
cauliflower cheese,
followed by peaches
DINNER:
chicken with vegetables,
followed by chocolate pudding

Astronaut **Owen Garriot** eating in space on board *Skylab*, 1973

As you can see, space food is pretty much the same as food here on Earth – it just comes in a different form.

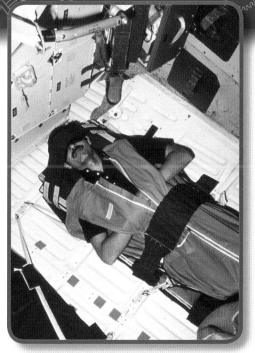

Sleep, But Not As We Know It

How can astronauts get a good night's sleep? By using **space-friendly bunk beds**, which don't take up too much room in the restricted craft. On the bunks are sheets with **microgravity restraints**, large straps that stop you from 'sleep floating'. There is also a headband to keep your head securely on the pillow. Space travelling can be extremely noisy, so earphones are a welcome extra.

If all the bunks are taken, you could snuggle down into a **space sleeping bag** instead. Hooked to the wall of the craft, these cosy bags prove that you can sleep just as well 'standing up' as lying down.

Shuttle astronaut in sleep restraint, 1980s

The **Orbital Workshop Waste Management Compartment**, 1972. Also known as the loo.

The 'Littlest Room' in Space

Astronauts today use a very effective 'space loo'. Rather than being flushed away with water, solid human waste is exposed to the vacuum of space, which sucks out all the moisture. What's left is compacted and stored, to be disposed of back on Earth – NOT in space, where there's enough junk floating around already!

To make use of the loo, you'll have to be fixed firmly on to the seat (restraining devices are provided). Make sure there are no gaps for anything to escape! Turn on the fan and you're away. Once the job is done, you seal up the top of the toilet and the powerful vacuum action takes place.

However tricky this sounds, it's an improvement on the early days of space travel when all astronauts had for a loo was a plastic bag attached to their rear end.

ALL DRESSED UP

As an astronaut you'll wear different clothes for different stages of your mission. Whatever you're doing, your outfits will be functional and comfortable – and some will be vital for your safety.

Flight Fashion

When travelling in a space shuttle you'll need to wear an **Advanced Crew Escape Suit** during the most dangerous times – launch and re-entry. This is the most likely time for an emergency bail-out to occur.

Alan Shepard, 1959. This is what astronauts wore in the early days.

Also known as the 'pumpkin suit' (bright orange will be seen more quickly in a rescue situation), it's equipped with all kinds of natty survival gadgets, from tools and mirrors to smoke flares. Some suits even have folded parachutes and inflatable life rafts attached to them.

Once your shuttle mission is established you'll change into a more comfortable **flight suit**. If you're staying at the space station, soft flexible clothes like t-shirts and tracksuit bottoms are usually worn. You'll find it handy to have lots of pockets to put things in to prevent them floating off. Velcro patches are also used for keeping objects such as tools firmly attached.

Spacesuit Style

Going out into space, whether you're working in the shuttle bay or walking on the moon, is another matter entirely. The atmosphere inside a spacecraft is fully pressurized, with oxygen for you to breathe and the right air pressure for the human body. But outside your craft you'll be exposed to intense cold, a complete lack of oxygen, dangerously low air pressure and harmful radiation. Your **spacesuit** is your own miniature pressurized environment. Without it, you would die.

Dr Mae Jemison wearing an Advanced Crew Escape Suit in 1992. Also known as the 'pumpkin suit'.

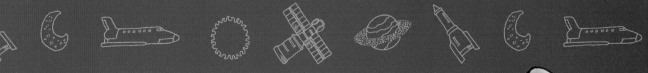

Spacesuit technology has improved enormously since the early days of space travel. Here's what the latest astronauts are wearing:

- Helmet contains a two-way radio, the tube to your water supply and a tinted visor to protect your eyes from the ultraviolet sunlight.

- You'll be wearing a special cloth hat under your helmet. This has headphones and a microphone attached to it so you can communicate with your colleagues effectively.

- Outer and inner gloves protect hands but offer some flexibility.

- Backpack contains oxygen supply, water, a ventilator to circulate oxygen round the suit, a filter to remove the carbon dioxide and moisture you breathe out, a pump to pump water around the suit to cool it and batteries that will keep it working for about seven hours.

- Underneath your suit you'll be wearing space underwear. It contains tiny tubes of water to keep you cool.

- Thick protective boots fasten on to the suit.

- Suit is made from several layers that keep you airtight and warm, and protect you from small micrometeoroid impacts.

Astro Fact

Space-walking astronauts are now able to wear jet-pack life jackets called SAFER. These enable them to fly back to the space station if they accidentally become untethered from the craft.

BACK TO EARTH

Congratulations! Your mission has been successfully completed and it's time to prepare for re-entry. The type of landing, or splash-down, will depend on what sort of craft you are travelling in.

Capsule

Despite the rocket's massive size, you will be travelling in a small capsule. In project *Apollo* it was called the **command module**. This sat on top of the service module, which contained instrumentation, life-support sytems and other supplies. Most of the rest of the rocket was divided into sections or stages, which contained giant fuel tanks. These sections soon fell away as the fuel was used up during the launch.

When the mission was nearing its end, the service module was jettisoned, leaving just the capsule to re-enter the Earth's atmosphere at a speed of 40,000 kmh (25,000 mph). All spacecraft re-entering the atmosphere heat up by hundreds of degrees Celsius as they squash the air in front of them, so capsules have thick heat shields for protection.

Parachutes are used to help slow the capsule once it has entered the atmosphere. There are then two ways of returning to Earth:

1. A **'splash-down'** into water
2. A **'touchdown'** on to land – the Russian way – retro rockets are fired just before landing to slow the capsule even more.

SPACECRAFT

1
2
3

THIRD STAGE

SECOND STAGE

FIRST STAGE

USA

Hopefully, you will have arrived back close to rescue crews, who will help you out of the capsule.

Gemini 9 **spacecraft after splashdown, 1966.** Astronauts Thomas Stafford and Eugene Cernan splashed down into the Atlantic Ocean on 6 June 1966 after a three-day mission in Earth orbit. They are shown here leaving the capsule with the assistance of divers.

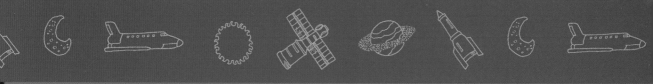

The *Apollo* space missions were launched by huge *Saturn* rockets in three sections. The space-craft is also divided into three sections:

1. Command Module – the only part to return to Earth

2. Service Module

3. Lunar Module containing the moon-landing craft

Shuttle Landing

These days, American astronauts mostly travel by space shuttle. You will be travelling in the orbiter (see page 22) at incredible supersonic (faster than sound) speeds of around 28,000 kph (17,000 mph). Slowing down is a precise business. You'll need to make some banking manoeuvres – four S-turns – and ensure the shuttle's wings are tipped at an exact angle to safely re-enter the atmosphere. A miscalculation could cause the shuttle to either burn up or skip back out of the atmosphere into space – and you won't have enough fuel left to try again.

Fortunately you'll have had plenty of practice beforehand on the shuttle simulator!

As the shuttle nears Earth a **parachute** is deployed from the back to help slow it down. The orbiter is then able to glide on to the runway without any engine power, using its wing and tail flaps for control.

Astro Fact

Some astronauts feel dizzy and have trouble walking once they've returned to Earth. This is caused by a temporary drop in blood pressure.

Space and the Atmosphere

The atmosphere is a layer of gases that surrounds Earth, protecting us from the Sun's ultraviolet radiation and extreme temperatures. Roughly 480 km (300 miles) thick, the atmosphere has no exact ending point; it just gets thinner and thinner until it fades away into space. Space is our name for the area that lies outside the Earth's atmosphere.

ADVENTUROUS ASTRONAUTS

Space technology continues to improve, enabling us to travel further and push back the boundaries of space exploration. So what new adventures might await astronauts of the future?

Mysterious Mars

One of the places that has long intrigued us is one of our nearest planets, **Mars**. We have sent many unmanned craft there over the years in order to gather information. But no human has ever set foot on the planet.

Why Haven't We Visited Mars Yet?

The main reasons are:

- **Money** – it would cost a huge amount, more than one nation could afford

- **Distance** – Mars is so far away that it would take an estimated two years to make the return journey

- **Conditions** – Mars has no magnetic field like Earth's, so astronauts would be exposed very high levels of radiation. And no one is sure how the human body would cope with such a long journey.

Scientists are working hard to overcome these incredible challenges and there is plenty of optimism about a future mission. The head of NASA has said he believes humans will set foot on Mars within thirty years. It's even possible that one of those first astronauts could be you ...

AstroFact

Some scientists have visualized the building of huge 'space cities' that could orbit Earth. These would provide artificial environments for communities of people to live in, with houses and trees, just like home.

Man on the Moon

Another idea is that we might one day live on the moon. The moon is much closer to Earth than Mars and we already know that a human can reach it. Even so, **colonizing** the moon would be a huge job. We'd need to construct an artificial world on its surface, with a controlled atmosphere and protection against radiation. Power could come from the sun and vegetables could be grown for food supplies. If we could achieve this goal, we might one day go on to colonize the rest of the solar system too.

A Holiday in Space

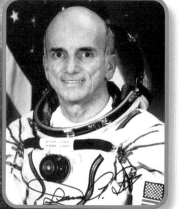

If you don't make it through astronaut training (and if you have enough cash), you could still perhaps visit space – by becoming a 'space tourist'. **Dennis Tito** was the first person to pay for a space flight, when he embarked on an eight-day mission to the ISS in 2001. The price? A mere twenty million US dollars. Luckily, Mr Tito was a multimillionaire. And his flight paved the way for the next generation of space adventurers, some of whom have already put down deposits for future trips. Several companies have set up in the business of space tourism and there are even plans for a launch of 'space hotels'.

Now you know everything you need to about becoming an astronaut. Still want the job? You bet!

Where can you entertain people of any age with **exhibitions**, **events**, **films**, **food** and **shops** – all under one roof, for anything from an **hour** to a **day**?

At the **Science Museum** you can do all this and much more. See iconic objects from **Stephenson's Rocket** to the *Apollo 10* command module, catch a **3D IMAX** movie, take a ride on our **simulators**, visit an **exhibition**, and encounter the past, present and future of **technology** in seven floors of **free** galleries, including the Museum's famous **hands-on galleries**, where children can have **fun** investigating **science** with our dedicated **Explainers** ... Whatever you do you won't be stuck for things to do at

the Science Museum.

science museum

Entry to the Museum is FREE, but charges apply to our IMAX cinema, simulators and special exhibitions. Family, discounted and combination tickets available. Call **0870 870 4846** for more information.

Science Museum, Exhibition Road, London SW7 2DD **www.sciencemuseum.org.uk**

Macmillan Children's Books is delighted to be publishing the following brilliant books in association with The Science Museum.

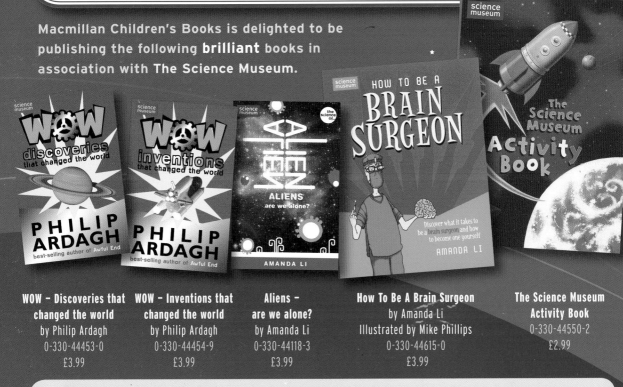

| **WOW – Discoveries that changed the world** by Philip Ardagh 0-330-44453-0 £3.99 | **WOW – Inventions that changed the world** by Philip Ardagh 0-330-44454-9 £3.99 | **Aliens – are we alone?** by Amanda Li 0-330-44118-3 £3.99 | **How To Be A Brain Surgeon** by Amanda Li Illustrated by Mike Phillips 0-330-44615-0 £3.99 | **The Science Museum Activity Book** 0-330-44550-2 £2.99 |

All **Pan Macmillan** titles can be bought from our website, **www.panmacmillan.com**, from the Science Museum Shop, or your local bookshop.

They are also available by post from: **Bookpost**, PO Box 29, Douglas, Isle of Man IM99 1BQ. Credit cards accepted. For details: telephone: 01624 677237, fax: 01624 670923, email: bookshop@enterprise.net, **www.bookpost.co.uk** Free postage and packing in the United Kingdom.